What Animal Is It?

by Pascal LaFontaine

HOUGHTON MIFFLIN   BOSTON

What has soft paws?

A cat has soft paws.

What has a curly pink tail?

A pig has a curly pink tail.

What has a pointy nose?

A fox has a pointy nose.

What has a beak?

A hen has a beak.

What has big feet
and says "Quack"?

A duck has big feet and says "Quack!"